A Day in the Life of an
Emergency Medical
Technician

Mary Bowman-Kruhm
and Claudine G. Wirths

The Rosen Publishing Group's
PowerKids Press™
New York

Thanks to Corporal Daniel D. Cornwell, President, National Flight Paramedics Association and 1996 Maryland Flight Paramedic of the Year, for his help with this book and to the Maryland State Police.

Published in 1997 by The Rosen Publishing Group, Inc.
29 East 21st Street, New York, NY 10010

Copyright © 1997 by The Rosen Publishing Group, Inc.

First Edition

Book Design: Erin McKenna

Photo Illustrations: Cover and all photo illustrations by Kelly Hahn.

Bowman-Kruhm, Mary.
    A day in the life of an EMT/ by Mary Bowman-Kruhm and Claudine G. Wirths.
        p.   cm. — (Kid's career library)
    Includes index.
    Summary: Describes the daily responsibilities and tasks that an EMT is ready to perform.
    ISBN 0-8239-5099-9
    1.Emergency medical technician—Juvenile literature. [1. Emergency medical personnel. 2. Occupations.]
I. Wirths, Claudine G. II. Title. III. Series.
RA645.5.B68 1997
610.69'53—dc21
                                             96-53132
                                                  CIP
                                                       AC

Manufactured in the United States of America

Contents

Trooper Dan Starts His Day

The station is busy when Trooper Dan Cornwell gets to work. He watches a **helicopter** (HEL-ih-kop-ter) land. A helicopter is also called a chopper.

"We took a sick baby to the **hospital** (HOS-pih-tul)," the **pilot** (PY-lut) tells Trooper Dan, as they walk into the station. Trooper Dan is an **emergency medical technician** (ee-MER-jen-see MED-ih-kul tek-NISH-un), or EMT. As he puts on his **uniform** (YOO-nih-form), Trooper Dan wonders, "Who will need our help today?"

◀ Trooper Dan is always ready to find and help sick or hurt people.

What Is Trooper Dan's Job?

Most EMTs work on the ground. But not Trooper Dan. Trooper Dan is a **flight paramedic** (FLYT par-ah-MED-ik). People can get help faster if they are flown to the hospital in a helicopter. The helicopter is like a flying emergency room. Trooper Dan is trained to be the eyes and ears and hands of a doctor while they are flying in the air. A doctor takes over when they land at the hospital.

Trooper Dan does most of his ▶
work inside the helicopter.

Ready to Go

The first thing Trooper Dan does each day is get the helicopter ready to fly. He washes it inside and out and then fills the tank with **fuel** (FEWL).

Next, he checks **supplies** (suh-PLYZ). Everything needed to help someone who is sick or hurt must be there.

Trooper Dan also checks the weather. There are no storms or strong winds today. The chopper is ready to go.

◀ One of the first things that Trooper Dan does is check that all of the medical supplies are in the helicopter.

Help!

Ring! Ring! A man on the phone says the police need EMT help. A boy fell while he was rock climbing with friends. Trooper Dan's **crew** (CROO) moves fast. They push the chopper out of its **hangar** (HANG-er). Trooper Dan checks his map for the place where they'll find the boy. The pilot climbs on board and starts the **engine** (EN-jin). The big blades turn around and around. They make a whirring sound. The pilot signals to Trooper Dan that he is ready to take off.

Trooper Dan is always ready to answer calls for EMT help. ▶

Takeoff

Trooper Dan is careful not to go behind the helicopter. He does not want to be hit by the blades. So he runs in from the front and keeps his head down. He jumps in his seat and fastens the belt. Slowly the helicopter moves up, up, up into the sky. The pilot sets the **controls** (kun-TROLZ) and the chopper starts to fly.

◀ The pilot prepares the helicopter for flight.

The Rescue

The pilot and Trooper Dan fly through the air and look for the boy. Soon Trooper Dan says, "I see him." The boy is lying on the ground. But there is nowhere to land.

"I'll go down and get him," says Trooper Dan. He checks the rope that holds the **stretcher** (STRECH-er). Then he takes the rope in one hand and holds on tight! He swings out on the rope and lowers himself to the ground. Trooper Dan straps the boy onto the stretcher. Then the pilot pulls them up into the helicopter.

Even if there is no place to land the helicopter, ▶
Trooper Dan will find a way to help someone.

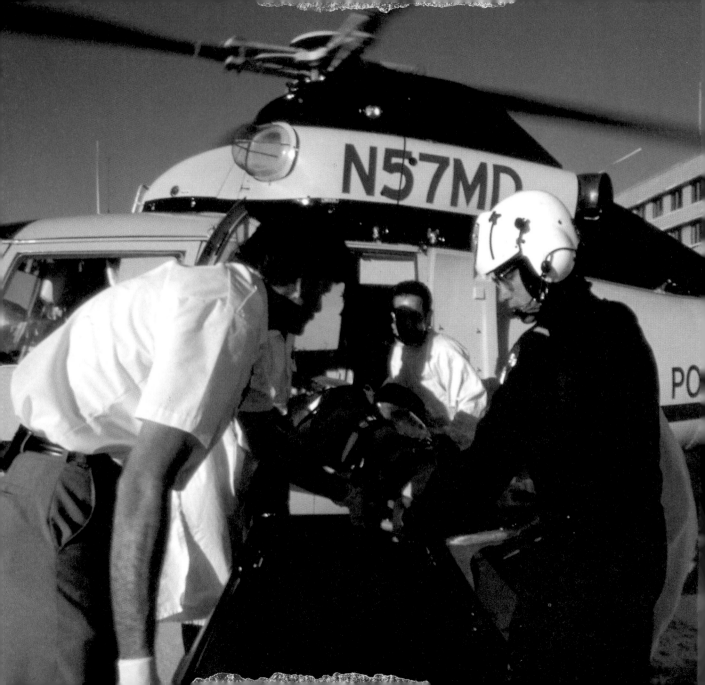

The Hospital

The pilot heads for the hospital. Trooper Dan talks to a doctor by radio while he checks the boy. The boy is in a lot of pain.

"His leg is broken," he tells the doctor on the radio. "Be ready."

The chopper lands and the hospital staff takes over. As Trooper Dan gets back in the helicopter, he hears a doctor say, "Trooper Dan got you here fast. Now we'll take care of you. You're going to be okay."

◀ As soon as the helicopter lands, a stretcher is ready to bring the hurt person into the hospital.

Another Call

The helicopter's radio crackles. Another call! Two men were hurt when their car ran into a pole. Trooper Dan cleans the helicopter while it's in the air to get it ready for the two men.

The pilot lands in a field near the highway. Trooper Dan and the pilot lift the men onto stretchers. One man has a bad cut on his arm. Trooper Dan stops the bleeding from the cut while the pilot flies them to the hospital.

Trooper Dan helps the hurt person as much as possible until the helicopter arrives at the hospital. ▶

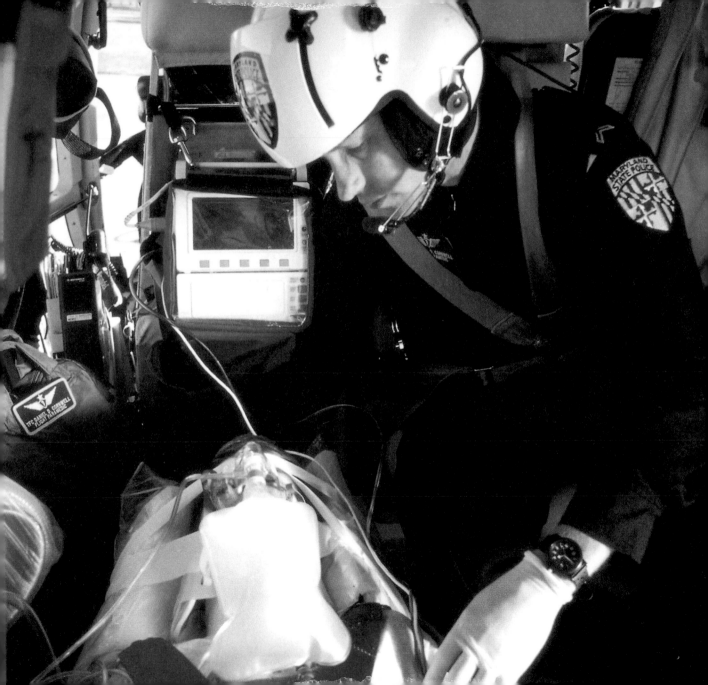

A School Visit to the Station

Back at the station again, Trooper Dan's crew gets the helicopter ready for the next call. While the crew works, Trooper Dan talks with some schoolchildren who visit the station. He tells the class what he has done today.

"Why do you like your job?" a boy asks.

"Saving someone's life makes me feel great," Trooper Dan says. "And the job is exciting."

"Can a girl be an EMT?" one girl asks.

"Anyone can be an EMT," says Trooper Dan.

◄ Anyone who is interested in medicine and wants to help people can be an EMT.

Trooper Dan Goes Home

At 7:00 that night, Trooper Dan's day is over. He goes home at last. He is glad that he and his crew were there to help people when they needed it. Now another EMT is on the job.

Trooper Dan hopes you will never be hurt or sick so that you need their help. But if you do, EMTs are ready.

Glossary

controls (kun-TROLZ) What the pilot uses to fly and guide the helicopter.

crew (CROO) A team of people working together to do a job.

emergency medical technician (ee-MER-jen-see MED-ih-kul tek-NISH-un), or **EMT** A person who takes care of sick or hurt people until they can get to a doctor.

engine (EN-jin) The motor that makes a chopper work.

flight paramedic (FLYT par-ah-MED-ik) An EMT who is trained to give hurt people emergency care while they are being flown to a hospital.

fuel (FEWL) A liquid that makes an engine or motor run.

hangar (HANG-er) A large building where airplanes and helicopters are kept.

helicopter (HEL-ih-kop-ter) A special kind of aircraft with blades on top that can fly straight up.

hospital (HOS-pih-tul) A place where sick or hurt people go to get well.

pilot (PY-lut) The person who flies a helicopter or plane.

stretcher (STRECH-er) A bed for carrying sick or hurt people.

supplies (suh-PLYZ) Things a person needs to do a job.

uniform (YOO-nih-form) Special clothes worn for a job.

23

Index